Balboa Press books may be ordered through booksellers or by contacting:

Balboa Press
A Division of Hay House
1663 Liberty Drive
Bloomington, IN 47403
www.balboapress.com
1 (877) 407-4847

Because of the dynamic nature of the Internet, any web addresses or links contained in this book may have changed since publication and may no longer be valid. The views expressed in this work are solely those of the author and do not necessarily reflect the views of the publisher, and the publisher hereby disclaims any responsibility for them.

Any people depicted in stock imagery provided by Getty Images are models, and such images are being used for illustrative purposes only. Certain stock imagery © Getty Images.

Library of Congress Control Number: 2016915593

ISBN: 978-1-5043-6418-8 (sc)
ISBN: 978-1-5043-6419-5 (e)

Print information available on the last page.

Balboa Press rev. date: 02/19/2018

BALBOA.
PRESS
A DIVISION OF HAY HOUSE

DAM IT!

JUST LET ME GRIEVE!

STOP THE PLATITUDES!
START THE GRIEVING!

JANA L. HERTZ

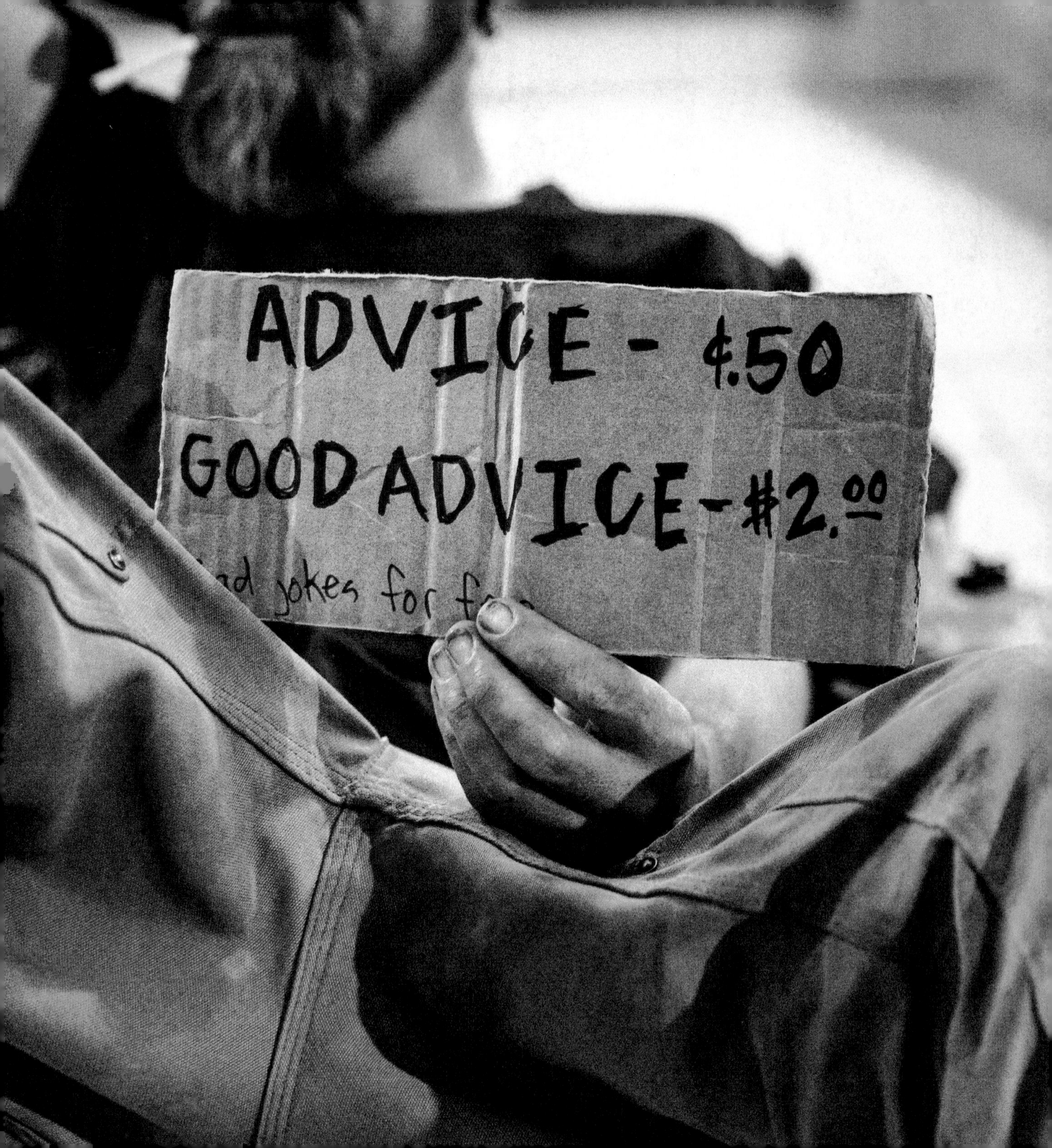
ADVICE - ¢.50
GOOD ADVICE - #2.00
jokes for

Advice is not nice!
What *not* to say

- "Snap out of it."
- "You shouldn't isolate."
- "Don't be sad; your loved one is with God."
- "Don't be sad; think of all the memories."
- "You've got to pull yourself through this."
- "At least they aren't suffering anymore."
- "Cheer up."
- "Be strong."
- "Get on with life."
- "It's time to stop grieving."
- "God should be your comfort."
- "You're still sad; your faith must not be strong."
- "I understand how you feel."
- "Remember we are never given more than we can handle."
- "It's God's will."
- "Call me if there's anything I can do." (they won't call; call them)
- "It was their time to die."
- "You must be strong for your children."
- "Time heals everything."
- "Try not to cry."
- "Everything will be okay."
- "Move On!"
- "They lived a long life!"
- "Get over it!" (No one ever gets over it!)

"Where grief is fresh, any attempt to divert it only irritates."

Samuel Johnson

Platitudes trigger attitudes!
Knee-jerk and wishful responses to grief advice:

- "Could you just shut the (bleep) up?"
- "Thanks for sharing your brilliance."
- "Wow! *THAT* was really comforting."
- "Would you mind if I punched you right now?"
- "Wow! Your compassion is astonishing!"
- "I can't believe you just said that to me! Really? Did you just hear yourself?"
- "How can you be so cruel?"
- "Did you really mean to say that to me?"
- "Be happy? What a great idea! Just stop being sad! Wow, thank you!"
- "Thanks, thanks so much."
- "It's not about you!"
- "I'm so sorry that the death of someone I love is inconveniencing you."

Outwardly, I handled everybody who used the usual trite missives with as much grace as I could manage, but inwardly, I was screaming, "DAMN IT, JUST LET ME GRIEVE!" I wanted to stifle their speech and yell, "Just shut UP!" The insipid proverbs added to my feelings of deep alienation, pushing me further into a place of dark, suffocating anguish. Clearly, people didn't know what to say; they were fumbling to connect and failing miserably. Grief and mortality frighten people, and when they don't know what to say, they fill the awkward silences with banal clichés.

Remember: Accept and encourage their grief journey, no matter how long it takes. It may take years. Ride the roller coaster with them. Judge not!

They don't get it? Don't sweat it!
Things to remember about those who aren't experiencing grief

- Grief frightens, disturbs, and alarms people

- Discomfort is obvious because it becomes about their comfort and not yours

- Culturally in America we don't allow for grief

- People mean well, so you may gently have to show them the way

When people respond inappropriately to your grief, you could say:

"I know you mean well and I know you dislike seeing me so sad, but I am on a grief journey and I would appreciate if you could just allow me to walk through my pain, no matter how long it takes."

For everything there is a season,
And a time for every matter under heaven:
A time to be born, and a time to die;
A time to plant, and a time to pluck up what is planted;
A time to kill, and a time to heal;
A time to break down, and a time to build up;
A time to weep, and a time to laugh.
A time to mourn, and a time to dance;
A time to throw away stones, and a time to gather stones together;
A time to embrace, and a time to refrain from embracing;
A time to seek, and a time to lose;
A time to tear, and a time to sew;
A time to keep silence, and a time to speak;
A time to love, and a time to hate;
A time for war, and a time for peace.

Ecclesiastes 3:1-8, *English Standard Version*

We are all familiar with these verses, whether heard in song or when repeatedly used at a variety of momentous occasions. These verses are reminders that life is full of joys and full of tragedies. No one is immune. Seasons come and seasons go; the circle of life remains.

"Everyone can master a grief but he that has it."

William Shakespeare

The Frail Trail: My Journey in Mourning

Death is pervasive; we all, unfortunately, are forced to confront mortality at some point in our lives. My first brushes with mourning came as a rapid-fire trio, beginning with the sudden death of my older brother, Kurt. Just six months later, I lost my father to cancer. Then, five days later, my dear friend Sally, a surrogate mother figure in my life, also passed away. My brother's death, being unexpected, floored me. Although I had expected my father's death, as his battle with cancer had been ongoing, and had zero regrets with it, the loss devastated me. My dad was my hero, and the fact that he was gone was too much for me to bear. I felt as if there was a dense weight upon me; even a year and a half after his death, I still struggled to get out of bed in the morning. The daily routine of my life was baffling, still, and I felt as if I had no purpose. During this period, I cried, constantly. I feared that my heart would be broken forever. I found solace in nothing, in nobody. I become something of a recluse. The only thing I wanted to do was lie in my bed and shut out the world. It may seem strange that I didn't reach out to my family, as they were grieving the losses of two of the very same people as I was, but at the time, this felt too vulnerable. I had not always felt at ease expressing myself in front of family members, so turning to them at this unprecedentedly devastating moment seemed daunting. To survive these losses, I isolated myself. I also felt as though I had nothing to give or offer them. I knew in my heart that my family was strong, and that they'd be okay. Reflecting on this period, I am reminded of the book of Matthew, in which Jesus fasts for 40 days, alone in the desert. Like His journey, this was one that I had to walk alone. In my heart, I believed that all people grieve uniquely, and that this had to be somehow acceptable.

My problem during this period was that I'd lost people I loved, and I'd never get them back. Fixing the problem was impossible, so it didn't really occur to me to rely on others for support. What could they possibly say to make it better? What could anybody do for me? I chose to sit in my despair, and let the world lurch forward without me. To me, those around me who weren't mourning were "whole." While I was not, I wanted these whole people to simply let me be. Looking back, this grief-clouded idea was far from reality.

After the first few months in my pit of misery, I forced myself to face the busy, productive world, and feign living. As a mother, my children required this of me, regardless of how I felt. This compelled me to interact with other people, which was dreadfully alienating. It made me angry. People said the damnedest things to me, and I wanted to scream at them, "DAMN IT! *Just let me grieve! Stop It! Stop saying hurtful things!"*

This phenomenon inspired me to write this book.

The aforementioned interactions with people frequently left me confused and hopeless. They seemed so awkward, and I felt as if I was being coerced into comforting them for my own loss. Why did my pain make them so uncomfortable? Why did they feel the need to say such inappropriate things? It occurred to me later that these well-intentioned people hated to see me so despondent and low. Perhaps they believed that if they gave me the proper shove, I'd shake myself out of it. Not knowing what to say, they fumbled along, unaware that their words were pushing me into a state of deeper isolation. They couldn't possibly comprehend how angry I was at the time, how I seethed under the surface, because I felt like I was being expected to stuff my feelings down inside for their benefit.

During this period of my life, I knew my friends and allies were watching me unravel and give up on living. This fear of judgment only caused me to want to sequester myself further and hide away. The responses that I'd get from them implied that I wasn't jumping through the hoops of Moving On quickly enough. It felt as if I was being judged for being weak because I stayed in bed all day. It all made me want to bury my head under the covers and hide, because on top of the inescapable pain of my losses, I was also *failing*, according to the outside world. It was as though I had a great, festering wound, and onlookers were rubbing salt into it. I had to ration my social interactions accordingly. I learned that when a wound heals slowly, people get uncomfortable.

Meanwhile, under the surface, I was losing my mind. On top of the incessant crying, I was tired and unable to concentrate. I stopped eating, began misplacing things and forgetting what I was doing or where I was going. Coping with the extreme feelings of loneliness and despair was difficult enough, and now I seemed unable to keep the thread of my daily life intact. I was terrified of this new set of difficulties that seemed to appear at the same time as my loss. I was unaware at the time that these, too, are all potential symptoms of the depression that comes with loss. My grief so altered my life and behavior that I eventually had to seek professional help, and even took antidepressants for a period of time. In counseling sessions, I was reassured that my outrageously divergent feelings and behavior were normal. Additionally, I was encouraged to read books on the subject of grief. The problem here was that since I had fallen into this depression, I had been virtually unable to read. My ability to focus and comprehend the written word appeared to be shattered, and as a lifelong avid reader, this freaked me out more than anything. All the books about mourning were heavy in content; they overwhelmed me. I longed for a basic, simple, book about the grieving process. I never did find that book.

It was this, combined with my thirst for more considerate support from well-meaning friends and acquaintances that compelled me to write this book.

Grief is mysterious and takes on its own form unique to both the life and the loss experienced. American culture is disturbingly lacking, when it comes to social allowances for grieving. We have no real ritual for it. When one loses a loved one, they are given a few days off from work, then expected to jump right back into the rat race- right back to the land of the living. The common sentiment seems to be, "You've buried your loved one, now bury your grief and move on." In many other cultures, rituals of grieving are socially acceptable; individuals are not only allowed, but *encouraged* to openly express their feelings, sometimes in gut-wrenching ways. Sometimes, the grieving is performed more privately, but time is set aside for it, and one is expected to use that time to mourn the loss. Outsiders know that the individual is in mourning, and don't treat them as if their emotions are inappropriate. In some cultures, one is allowed to lie in their pain, and others understand that in due time, they will eventually recover and resume regular life. Losses must be processed properly, not masked.

Another example of mourning is Job, of the Bible. Job lost his wealth, his servants, and all of his children in one fell swoop. Just consider that- he lost *everything*. When Job's three friends heard of his losses, they came to him in order to mourn with him. They tore their clothes, and sprinkled ashes atop their heads. Then, they sat with Job in silence for seven days and seven nights, because they understood that his grief was so incomprehensible, words would be useless. Unfortunately, Job's friends later offered up unnecessary rhetoric to make sense of Job's devastation. To them, he replies, "I have heard all this before. What miserable comforters all of you are!" (*The Living Bible,* Job 16:2) The actions of Job's friends serve as prime examples of things to do and things not to do. Sit with the bereaved in silence and allow them as much time as they need, but don't try to make sense of their loss for them or tell them how to feel.

"But grief is a walk alone. Others can be there, and listen. But you will walk alone down your own path, at your own pace, with your sheared-off pain, your raw wounds, your denial, anger, and bitter loss. You'll come to your own peace, hopefully…. but it will be on your own, in your own time."

Cathy Lamb

"He heals the broken hearted, and binds up their wounds...

The Lord supports the afflicted."

Psalm 147:3 & 6, *New American Standard Bible*

"Every life has a measure of sorrow, and sometimes this is what awakens us."

Steven Tyler

Grief is pervasive; it is how we choose to cope with it that can make all the difference in our lives, our communities, and in the world. Loss and its consequences in America can also be collective, from the terrorist attacks on September 11th, 2001, to Hurricane Katrina, to school shootings like Columbine High School in 1999 and Sandy Hook, in 2012. The world at large is steeped in loss, courtesy of natural disasters and ongoing wars, and it never stops. Even Jeanne Philips, the real-life author of the "Dear Abby," column, has been repeatedly asked by her readers about how to cope with loss and grief, so there is a demonstrable need to distill the complexities of grieving into an easier-to-grasp set of realities. On a more subtle level, grief can fill our lives often and fully, yet remain socially taboo. The masses squirm at its mention and it seems a perpetual elephant in the room, so to speak. The losses of relationships, jobs, aspirations, ideals, pets, homes, and health, can also be mourning experiences in our lives. These losses can knock us off-kilter, leaving us in an unexpectedly complicated state, perplexed by our feelings. Grieving is a natural process of life, yet it often feels unnatural, gut-wrenching, and raw. When grief uppercuts us, it is imperative to allow ourselves to process it, in order to heal, and learn to live with the scar the loss leaves behind. For those who feel lost on their personal path through mourning, my deepest hope is that you will be comforted in some manner by the words in this book, or at the very least, understand that you aren't alone. Realizing that your grief can be processed in healthy ways will enable you to resume a more productive, joyful life, while learning to balance the lasting void left behind by your loss. It *is* possible!

Landing the understanding

Grief/griːf/*noun*/
1. Keen mental suffering or distress over affliction or loss; sharp sorrow; painful regret.
2. A cause or occasion of keen distress or sorrow.

   Grief is a response to an experience of loss

<u>Synonyms:</u>

1. Anguish, heartache, woe, misery; sadness, melancholy, moroseness, sorrow.

Dictionary.com Unabridged (v 1.0.1)
Based on the Random House Unabridged Dictionary, © Random House, Inc. 2006.

There are a variety of losses that we may endure during a lifetime.

The loss of:

- A loved one
- A beloved pet
- A job, career or promotion
- A marriage or relationship
- A home
- Dreams, aspirations, and ideals
- Sentimental objects
- Surroundings (changes in residences, schools, work places)
- Health or ability
- Identity (due to physical, emotional, mental, financial, and/or spiritual abuse)
- A pregnancy
- Financial stability
- Normality, due to natural disasters, plane crashes, terrorist attacks, wars, and much, much more.
- A season in your life (kids moving out of the home, retirement, etc.)

Note: Grief can also affect people in other situations, for example, recipients of transplant organs often feel survivor's guilt, a kind of grief, knowing that another person died so that they could live. People who live through disasters, soldiers who serve during wartime, and those who survive accidents experience survivor's guilt. Additionally, new parents can experience grief when a pregnancy has unexpected results, such as a baby born with special needs.

Particular losses can seem insignificant, silly, or even ridiculous to others, giving the message that we shouldn't feel so badly or even grieve at all. Grieving is not something many people want to deal with at any level because anything that isn't positive, fun, or happy is shunned. Anything that seems unpleasant is set aside.

However, loss *must* be dealt with because, if not, it resurfaces with a vengeance and wreaks havoc in the sufferer's life. Death and loss surround us, and hopefully, this little book will assist you on your journey as a mourner, or as a friend who is looking to be supportive. It may even provide guidance that will be relevant in dealing with losses you experience in the future. Being alive, being a person, means that grief is, unfortunately, inevitable.

It's *crucial* to realize that comparing grief is futile. Grief is grief. Quantifying it serves little purpose and does not bring comfort in the long run. Although someone may have experienced "more" loss than others, it does not minimize the grief of someone who has lost "less." Honoring and heeding grief as others travel through its tangled complexities requires the expression of both grace and empathy.

> **"No matter what anybody says about grief and about the healing of all wounds, the truth is, there are certain sorrows that never fade away until the heart stops beating and the last breath is taken. Grief changes shape, but it never ends."**
> **-Keanu Reeves**

"It requires more courage to suffer than to die."

Napoleon Bonaparte

Grief is not brief
Grief is:

- Powerful
- Slow-moving
- Inevitable! It feels unnatural, however, it *is* natural to experience death and loss during the duration of our life
- Overwhelming
- Physically painful
- Capable of catching one off guard, knocking them to their feet, and shaking them to their core
- An indescribable pain that can be felt physically, emotionally, socially, mentally, and spiritually
- Jolting and staggering
- A process that can leave one feeling hopeless or meaningless
- Something that can compel one to believe that they've lost their center
- Unexpected, sometimes, such as when one hears a particular song, smells a reminiscent fragrance, hears a poignant story, or stumbles upon a photo
- Often triggered by specific holidays and seasonal traditions, as well as anniversaries of significant events
- Shocking, disorienting, and complicated
- Traumatic
- Messy and confusing
- Not fixable--it's a lifelong process

"Grief makes one hour ten."

William Shakespeare

The attributes of grief
Fazed, dazed and crazed

After my personal losses, I truly thought that I was losing my mind! I was exhibiting signs and symptoms consistent with the grieving process, but didn't understand this at the time. The books on the subject that I tried to read were no help, as they were so wordy and deep that they overwhelmed me. I was scared because my ability to read and concentrate was so drastically affected, as well. All I really needed at the time was to be reassured that my symptoms were indeed due to the intense psychological effects of loss, and be validated and told that whatever emotions I happened to be feeling were okay. It was really relieving to know, eventually, that I was, in fact, pretty normal, in my grieving state.

I definitely felt like I was going insane, sometimes. When I happened upon a particular quote by the acclaimed actress, Helen Hayes, speaking about the death of her beloved husband, I was oddly comforted. She said, "I was just as crazy as you can be and still be at large. I didn't have any normal moments during those two years. It wasn't just grief; it was total confusion. I was nutty."

Feeling and dealing
Shades of grief

- **Numbness and denial:** You may feel shock or disbelief and operate for a time on "autopilot."

- **Anger and protest:** You may feel angry and want to feel in control of something, or lash out at others. Physically, you might cry, feel weak, experience nausea, loss of appetite, or sleep disturbances.

- **Depression, Isolation, or despair:** Deep anguish and fatigue may manifest and you may feel the need to hide away from your life, or as if life cannot or should not continue without the person you've lost, which can result in compounded feelings of isolation.

- **Bargaining and detachment:** A mourner may obsess about specific aspects of the death. Additionally, the mourner may at some point begin detaching from it altogether. They may disengage, in an attempt to make sense of life without the person they've lost.

- **Acceptance and recovery:** The loss will eventually seem lighter, and the feeling of hurt will lessen with time. The bereaved begins healing, remembering the nuanced, positive and negative qualities of the person who died.

You may vacillate between all the shades of grieving, or just experience two or three. You may move out of one, into another, and back again. There is no time limit to grief. Acceptance does not mean you've found closure necessarily; perhaps you have just learned how to cope and live with it. Remember, grieving is a process. You will never simply, "get over it."

"If you suppress grief too much it can well redouble."

Moliere

Embrace the woe, then let it go

Do:

- Cry, sob and weep
- Express anger in an appropriate manner
- Sleep and rest
- Nourish yourself
- Ask for what you need
- Lie in the sun or sit in the rain (Or vice-versa!)
- Be forgiving of yourself
- Watch television (I repeatedly watched reruns of my dad's favorite shows, over and over)
- Listen to music
- Read
- Write, journal, and record your thoughts and feelings
- Sit and vegetate
- Utilize creative outlets (e.g., make a scrapbook, write a poem, do memorializing art projects, etcetera) **Note:** you may not feel up to this right away, and that's okay! Be patient with yourself!
- Exercise, even if it's just simple stretches
- Pace yourself
- Allow yourself to feel your pain: cry, scream, sleep, reminisce, and express yourself, even when it seems strange or difficult
- Create a memorial (Living memorials, such as planting a tree, can be healing)
- Pamper yourself
- Attend a grief support group and confide in those who can relate to you
- Connect daily with a person who has earned your trust
- Meditate and practice mindfulness. If faith is something you practice, spend time in prayer, talking openly and honestly with God
- Protect yourself; you are not obligated to be expressive or vulnerable on demand
- Seek grief counseling
- Practice self-care: grief is an extensive and slow process that unfolds in tender layers
- Pursue any form of therapy that you feel would be beneficial and meet your needs- animal, music, and art therapy can be powerful, for example

Essentially, do whatever you are feeling, no matter how absurd or difficult it seems! What works for one person may not work for somebody else.

Remember: Everyone grieves differently

Remember:

Grief is mysterious and takes on its own form.

Grief- the deep sting that does its thing
Symptoms of grief can include, but are not limited to:

- Forgetfulness, clumsiness, and confusion (While driving, I would forget where I was headed. I dropped things constantly, and bumped into things while walking.)

- Disorganization and confusion (I locked my keys in the car four times in a row!)

- Fatigue and sleep disruptions (I felt exhausted, barely able to put one foot in front of the other, as if my feet were lead. All I wanted to do was fall asleep and never awaken.)

- Preoccupation with the loss (I'd wear a favorite flannel shirt that had belonged to my dad, and his white tube socks- anything that kept him wrapped around me. My brother almost always wore a baseball cap, so we had memorial caps made for his service; I wore mine often, as well.)

- Feelings of despair and lack of motivation (I was listless, and would sit for hours. Mentally, I could barely grasp even simple tasks, such as eating, getting out of bed, or showering.)

- Heightened emotional sensitivity and weepiness (I wept so much and so often that I surprised myself. I cried excessively!)

- Reduced focus and retention (As I mentioned on a previous page, I struggled with reading for the first time in my life, and this lasted for two-and-a-half years. Interestingly, crossword puzzles replaced reading and gave me some small relief, keeping my mind occupied.)

- Changes in appetite (While grieving, food stopped appealing to me, and I lost weight.)

- Stress (I felt stressed because during my grief period, I was absent from my kids' lives, and they were used to having a mother who was present and capable. I felt guilt and shame because I wasn't snapping out of it.)

- Physical pain (I was so anguished that my chest felt constricted, and my stomach was perpetually in knots. I sought professional help, opting to take antidepressants for about a year, until I felt stable enough to wean myself off of them under a doctor's supervision.)

- Unpredictable or contradictory emotions (I experienced emptiness, irritability, guilt, panic, relief, heartache, and numbness, each emotion swirling in me like a tornado that dropped its cargo at random.)

- Peaks and Valleys (I was in the valley for a long time, before I was able to even grasp the idea of a peak.)

- For me, these symptoms were present to a profound degree. However, you may experience some of these symptoms and not experience others. You may experience things that aren't even listed here or very little symptomatic grief at all. Remember, everyone grieves differently.

Remember: If the intensity, frequency, and duration of your grief symptoms become extreme or overwhelming, seek out appropriate professional guidance. If you are experiencing thoughts of suicide, or you are concerned that a person in your life might be thinking about suicide, seek emergency medical assistance immediately.

"Tearless grief bleeds inwardly."

Christian Nevell Bovee

Don't smother or cover
Don't:

- Mask your grief with alcohol, drugs or harmful substances

- Make major decisions like moving, getting a new job, etc. (If you must, seek a professional who can guide you appropriately.)

- Isolate yourself completely for any longer than a month

- Try to act as if you are not grieving

- Expect anybody to understand your grief or heal it for you. They can't.

- Stay quiet about the needs you have at any given moment; be communicative

- Remain locked in an extreme state of grief for a long period of time; seek professional guidance if you need it

- Expect yourself to simply "get over it," at some point, because it doesn't work that way.

It's great to relate
Making a connection

When I was walking through my own valley of grief, I was surprised to find that I felt comforted when I heard others describe their own experiences with loss. I hated that they, too, had to feel such a singular pain, but it was still bracing, to understand that I wasn't alone. A poignant example of this comes to mind, when I remember seeing Gwyneth Paltrow on television, a guest on the Oprah Winfrey Show. She was speaking about having recently lost her father, and she was expressing so many of the intense emotions that I was feeling at the time, that I felt like I could have related to her in this way. In those minutes on the screen, I felt like we understood each other, because although her relationship with her dad was very different from mine, we were both grieving daughters. She was not just Gwyneth Paltrow, larger-than-life actress; she was a grieving daughter, too.

The following is an excerpt from the transcript of that particular Oprah Winfrey Show.

WINFREY: I had read that when your father passed, that you thought you would never get up off of your knees.
Ms. PALTROW: Yeah.
WINFREY: Yeah.
Ms. PALTROW: Yeah, I did. I mean, my father was the one person in my life who was like the center. I mean, he was always the person, you know, you would call for advice, for help, for a salad recipe, for a laugh, for whatever. I mean, he was everything. And I really--there were few mornings where I really thought that I was going to just die from the grief. Like I felt like, you know how you hear about animals, when they're wounded; they go off to die under a bush. I really---I connected with that feeling, like I- there were a few mornings where I thought I wasn't going to get through it.
WINFREY: You said you'd wake up and be surprised that you were still here breathing.
Ms. PALTROW: Yes, I just couldn't believe it. I just woke up again, and you know. And yeah, I just kept waking up, so I had to keep going and …
WINFREY: And how did you get through it?
Ms. PALTROW: You know, I talked to a therapist, and, like did grief counseling and read grief books and you do what you can. Nothing really helps.
WINFREY: Nothing helps. I hear it. You just walk through the pain.
Ms. PALTROW: Yeah, you just walk through it.

Thank you, Ms. Paltrow, for your courage to be vulnerable and for sharing your anguish so openly. I know I felt connected to you in that moment and became less vulnerable in my grief. I am certain that others did also. That's what it is all about; connecting and helping others cope in their journey to heal their grief.

Remember:

Everyone grieves differently.

"Grief drives men into habits of serious reflection, sharpens the understanding and softens the heart."

John Adams

Remember:

There is no time limit to grief.

"I loathe a friend whose gratitude grows old, a friend who takes his friend's prosperity, but will not voyage with him in his grief."

Euripides (Greek playwright)

Mindful sincerity invites clarity
Things to say to those who grieve:

- "I'm so sad about _____'s death. I miss them every day." Name the person!
- "I can't imagine your pain; my heart aches for you."
- "If you need to talk, I will listen." **And then just listen**.
- "You are in my thoughts and prayers."
- "Your feelings must be overwhelming; please take it one step at a time."
- "You have my deepest condolences/sympathies over the death of _____." Name the person!
- "Take all the time you need."
- "I don't know what to say, but I am here and I care."
- "You are loved."
- "I embrace you and what you are going through."
- If you aren't sure what to say, ask.

Reminders:

- Be compassionate and show sincere empathy.

- Simply ask if they want to talk about their loved one. If so, just listen. If not, just sit quietly with them. Silence is golden. Allow them to take the lead. Often they may simply wish to chat about a variety of things.

- If an intense emotion is expressed by someone in grief, allow it to flow from them. Just be present, and remember that you don't need to try and fix it for them in any way. Instead, choose to feel flattered; this person clearly feels safe enough with you to vent and emote.

The "do's" are not about you
Do: Make sure gestures are appropriate to the depth of the relationship

- Expect nothing from the person grieving. Just be there.

- Always make your contact with them be about them and not you.

- Send a card and keep it simple. Less is more. "I'm thinking of you" is sufficient.

- Call. Keep it brief, but sincere.

- When proposing anything, always give them a choice. (e.g., "Let's have coffee together. Is Thursday at 10:00 better for you, or Friday at 8:00?") **Apply this strategy to any of the following suggestions.**

- Offer to change the linens on beds to prepare for out of town guests.

- Ask if you can pick up or drop off any items that may need to be dry cleaned in preparation for the memorial.

- Make yourself available to pick up any out-of-town guests who arrive at the airport in order to attend services.

- Offer to answer the phone, take messages, and screen calls.

- Simple, personal gifts such as artwork, journals, and thoughtful playlists burned onto a "CD can be comforting.

- Crowd source 30 days of meals, along with teas and coffees. Meals can be gifted in freezer-safe containers, for hassle-free reheating. Soups are great! Keep it simple; take cheeses, deli meats and a variety of breads and condiments. Add breakfast foods, such as cereals, muffins, and jams. Add in paper goods for easy disposal.

- Drop off snacks. Often, the bereaved are hosting family and other guests.

- Offer to take their kids or pets for the day. You can take them to play at the park, or plan another fun activity.

- Offer to pick up groceries and put them away.

- Offer to clean their home, or pay to have it professionally cleaned.

- Offer to wash their car, bringing all necessary items with you.

- Treat them to a spa day, pedicure, or manicure. Allow them to go solo, if they'd' prefer.

- Call occasionally to remind them that they aren't forgotten. If they don't pick up, leave a simple message, like, "Hey, I just wanted to let you know that I'm thinking of you today." A simple, "I love you," can be comforting. Even if they don't often call back, it's never personal.

- Make them a mini scrapbook about their loved one. Heartfelt memories usually bring a sense of comfort.

- Write down a special memory of their loved one and share it with them via email or letter. Keep it short and sweet.

- Verbally share a warm memory of their loved one, at an appropriate moment.

- Be mindful with the usual condolences and adages. Avoid using words like, "should" and, "need"

- Spruce up flower arrangements and remove any dead blooms.

- Remember the date of their loved one's death. In the years to come, make sure to call, send them a note, or take them out.

- Invite those grieving to your functions. They may not attend for awhile but knowing they were included brings comfort!

- Give them this book.

Remember:

If you are receiving a kind gesture from someone, receive it graciously; it is a gift for you both!

"**Asking for support from the right people at the right time helps you summon the courage to show more of who you are to the world.**"

Rhonda Britten

Lend a sincere ear to hear
The Greatest Gift: loving by listening

Just being present for those grieving is a gift. It's about being totally available to those wading through mourning, rather than sounding off the correct remark of condolence or filling the awkward, often distressing silences with idle chatter.

Practice listening from the heart:

- Embrace their silence. Sit alongside them.
- Just hang together and don't force sharing.
- Allow them to feel safe in your presence.
- Look them in the eyes when they share from their heart.
- Empathize with them.
- Concentrate on their words.
- Allow them to talk about anything without interruptions from you.
- Respond by nodding, which acknowledges that you are hearing.
- Give them your full attention.
- Keep encouraging them to share by asking them simple questions.
- Ask permission to share something if you think it would comfort them, but tread lightly!
- Less is more; relate simply so there is no dominating the conversation to make it be about your story.
- Embrace their emotions and allow them to flow forth.
- Show up for them as often as they need, even if they repeat things over and over. The need to be heard is vital.
- Don't be timid; use the deceased's name in conversation. They existed and lived, so it's okay (and often comforting) to speak about them. Refusing to use their name is to, essentially, erase them.
- Allowing the conversation to go their way is ultimately the best road to travel. More than likely, it will move in and out of a variety of topics, each with its own emotional charge.

Forge spaces for grief's faces
Grief is a family affair
Realize that women, men, and children each grieve uniquely

- *Stereotypically,* women tend to express their emotions more freely than men do. Usually, women are the "feelers" and are more comfortable expressing their grief in a demonstrative fashion.

- *Stereotypically,* men tend to avoid expressing their emotions as openly as women do. Men are action-oriented, and often prefer problem solving to emoting, especially in front of others. Men typically want to appear "strong", and can seem detached, or cold. They may cope with loss by throwing themselves into a project or their work. Any tears shed, may be in private settings.

- Children grieve just as deeply as adults do, but express themselves in direct correlation to their cognitive and developmental ability. Encourage children to freely articulate themselves in any way that feels comfortable to them, and remember that they will respond to the honesty of the situation. Including children in the death and bereavement rituals surrounding a death gives them useful context for processing loss in the future, and enables them to cope more effectively. Always assure them that their feelings are accepted.

- **NOTE:** remember that grief expression can and often does deviate from stereotypical norms of gender. There is no correct or incorrect way for a man or woman to grieve based on their gender.

- Additionally, it's important to remember that each family member will grieve differently. It's also vital to keep the lines of communication open, and to let everybody involved in a death know that their individual processing is acceptable.

- In the wake of a death, some families fall apart, while others seem to band together. Just as each individual grieves uniquely, each family grieves uniquely. We can't control how our family members feel or process a loss, but we can do our best to communicate love and support, as well as our own needs, in the hope that our families remain tight-knit through a difficult death experience. Sometimes this is not the case and unfortunately, couples who lose a child often separate or divorce.

- In the event of the breakdown of a family's bonds, remaining open is key. Have faith that each family member will eventually, with time, find their way home, making space for a healthy closeness to rekindle. The bonds between family members can even be strengthened through adverse experiences.

- Further, it bears noting that sometimes, a person who was recently widowed may move rather quickly into a new romantic relationship. This can seem confusing, even hurtful, to onlookers who are also still grieving the loss of their partner. It's good to try and remember that they never stop loving the person who died, even while they open their heart to a new person who may come after. Love expands, which enables us to love all of our children, spouses, friends, and family members. When we lose a friend, we don't stop spending time with our other friends, and we also develop new friendships as our lives continue forward. Humans are fully capable of celebrating the past while simultaneously embracing both the present and the future.

History and Mystery; Grief can be surprising

Each of the three significant deaths to which I have alluded in the text of this book affected me in unique and unexpected ways. The first, the death of my brother, was a sudden death that nobody was anticipating. In the immediate wake of the news, the knowledge that he had died in an ambulance, surrounded by strangers, plagued me to the point of feeling physically ill. My family converged on my sister's house, which was a long drive for me to make with my kids. On my arrival, all I felt the ability to do was sleep, which I did for two or three days. After that, I summoned the will power to join my family in planning his service, and I immediately dove into creating a memory scrapbook in his honor. Having something meaningful to contribute gave me the energy to cope, and afforded me a sense of control over something which was extremely helpful in those first days. However, I felt a deep sense of sorrow and regret, because of the many things I wanted to say to him and wasn't able to, due to the manner and suddenness of his death.

After we lost my brother, my dad's cancer took its toll. He plummeted rapidly after losing his son. In a matter of months, we were saying our final goodbyes to him as well. In contrast to the loss of my brother, I knew I had expressed everything that I needed to, to my dad. We were both at complete peace with each other, and I had no regrets. Although I had been *dreading* his death for some time, I figured I'd get through it the same way I'd gotten through my brother's death; I'd do something constructive, send him off with a beautiful tribute, and feel some semblance of closure. I believed that in the wake of my dad's death, I could maintain that sense of control. My expectations completely missed the mark. If mourning my brother was like falling down, and having the wind knocked out of me, losing my dad was like being hit by a freight train. I didn't anticipate at all the deep spiral of depression that would befall me when I lost him, nor could I have predicted the mental breakdown that would color my life for several years afterward. I have since learned that this breakdown and depression were a cumulative sort of grief— I was grieving the three major deaths I'd just experienced, in addition to every single loss that I'd incurred in my life and hadn't allowed myself to process, before then.

A mere five days after the death of my father, my friend Sally died in her sleep. She had been my mentor, mother figure, and close friend for 24 years. I'd known her since I was a teenager, and she'd touched my life profoundly during that time. Her death, being completely unanticipated, immersed me in shock and denial. I believe now that my body could not physically handle the toll of another death, and that this is why I compartmentalized Sally's loss immediately. This compartmentalization was startling to me, since before this point, I'd never compartmentalized anything before. I'd always been free with my feelings, and this was the first moment of my life that seemed like a stark departure from who I'd always been. It took me a number of years to begin unpacking Sally's death. Eventually, memories of her began to pop up with increasing frequency and I began writing about her, which enabled me to start processing.

My experience, losing three deeply significant people in my life, in rapid succession, taught me that grief is mysterious and that nothing adequately prepares you for it. I vacillated through the different symptoms and phases of grieving, seemingly at random. I moved between numbness, deep despair, and isolation, with little rhyme or predictive reason. Attempting to map out personal grief will only create frustration, and much of that will be targeted within. It's important to be gentle with ourselves and cede control: grief is mysterious and unprecedented.

Out of night- into light
Healing:

- Is a choice

- Occurs while walking through the anguish and pain of your grief

- Begins inside before moving outward

- Seeps slowly into the painful crevices when active mourning is permitted

- Happens amidst the deep pain of loss

- Transpires when you respect your feelings

- Requires courage

- Takes time

- Comes to pass when you allow your reactions to flow unhindered

- Takes effect even when falling apart; doing so allows you to potentially arise as a healthier, stronger person

Remember:

- Time is neutral.
- Time does not heal grief.
- What you do with your time is what matters.
- Recovery is a choice.

REMEMBER:

There is no time limit to grief.

A new lease on peace
Hope

- Gradually, you will reawaken and come back to yourself.

- Incrementally, you'll reconnect with friends, routines, and leading a purposeful life. It happens in stages.

- Slowly, your energy and positivity will return.

- With time, you *will* see the light at the end of this dark tunnel.

- Little by little, the emotional extremes will lessen.

- At some point, you will begin reaching out to others.

- Bit by bit, the intensity of your anguish will diminish, and your ability to focus will come back.

- One day, the wound will feel less raw, and you'll become stronger and healthier.

- Your journey through grief will change you forever, leaving an emotional scar, however, the wound can heal.

- Grieving is a process- allow it.

- Remember: You will *never* simply "get over it," and that's okay.

Remember:

Sometimes the wound heals, but the scar remains forever.

"Death ends life, not the relationship."

Morrie Schwartz

If you've been paying attention so far, you know how much my father meant to me, and how devastated I was when I lost him. However, for most of my life, our relationship was complicated and painful. My dad was verbally, physically, and emotionally abusive when I was a child. At some point during my 30's, I cut him off entirely. During that period, he called me every month and asked if he could take me out to dinner. Month after month, I replied with a firm, "no!" I fully expected him to grow tired of my contempt, become angry, and give up. He didn't and it surprised me into a reluctant agreement, approximately a year into our standoff. At dinner, he shared a great deal with me, including the ways in which he knew he had failed as a father. He expressed that he had been reflecting on the many painful experiences of his own life, and that had left him the angry, volatile man I'd always known. He wasn't playing the victim; he was simply being open with me, assuming responsibility for the damage he'd left in my life. I was flabbergasted that he had been seeking professional help for three years! While I didn't expect him to behave this way, I still distrusted his motives. To test him, I spoke about the harrowing journey of my then-recent divorce, and in great detail, related the choices I'd been making, in order to cope with it. Many of these choices were rebellious in nature, in that they didn't fit in at all with my conservative Christian upbringing; I was angry and felt fed up with always doing the "right," things I'd been taught to do, since those things hadn't insulated me from a failed marriage. I expected my dad to judge me, to judge my decisions, but instead, he simply repeated, "I still love you," over and over again, no matter what I said. No judgment, no lectures, and no manipulation whatsoever.

I was floored. Who was this man? My dad had changed. The decade that followed our dinner together was one of the most prolific periods of my life; he truly was the dad I'd always wished for. He eventually came to be my hero. Over time we healed together, and the experience was life changing in instrumental ways, for me. My choices going forward, with my dad's honest and unconditional love in my heart, began an extreme shift. I shudder at the thought that I might have again said, "no" that night. If I'd chosen to keep shutting him out, I would have missed out on the most healing evening of my life. I'd never had a hero before; he supported me through many difficult experiences during the following decade. He proved to me that people *can* change, provided that they choose to. At age 72, when lung cancer took him from me, I lost the most powerful person in my life. I'd finally gotten my hero, and our time together was too short, in that sense. Even as I write this page, the tears flow, and I feel a pain in my chest that throbs. The choice to forgive my dad left me profoundly changed forever, and losing him altered me even further. I wasn't the same after I lost him, and I never will be.

I will never view life the same way, nor will I ever stop missing him. In my heart, there is, and always will be, a void where my father once stood. It is accompanied by the gulfs left behind by Kurt, my big brother, and Sally, my beloved friend. I coped, and I live my life around their absences, but I'll never *get over* it.

"Blessed be the God and Father of our Lord Jesus Christ, the Father of mercies and God of all comfort; who comforts us in all our affliction so that we may be able to comfort those who are in any affliction with the comfort with which we ourselves are comforted by God."

II Corinthians 1:3-4, *New American Standard Bible*

In memory of:

Kurt D. Eichmeyer
February 27, 1955–May 16, 2003

My big brother, my protector, my adorer
He walked a hard life, yet found laughter in the small things.
Always ready to celebrate, always wearing a hat, so young at heart.
I miss you and my birthday will never be the same
without your early morning phone call.

William Don Eichmeyer
September 18, 1931– November 9, 2003

My dad, my hero, my example
He walked with God, fought his demons, and demonstrated redemption.
One is never too old to choose change!
Thanks for loving me unconditionally and steadfastly.
Life without you is agony, but I find peace
when I remember that we'll be reunited someday.

Sally Johnson Hahne
July 17, 1937–November 14, 2003

My kindred spirit, my prayer warrior, my life-long champion
She lived her life charitably, her unique capacity to embrace others so genuinely and effortlessly,
extended consistently through cards, letters, phone calls, visits, and prayers.
A zest for life that was infectious.
An inspiration to all who were blessed to know and love her.
She unequivocally believed in me and knew my heart,
so I know she is applauding my journey to take joy in living just as she did daily.

It's been 14 years since I lost my dad, brother, and friend. Since those losses, I have encountered death a number of times. I have lost my sister-in-law, Debi. I lost my cousins, Mark and Fred. I lost my Uncle John and Aunt Virginia. Most recently, I was forced to say goodbye to my mother. Just a few weeks before her 82nd birthday, she abruptly fell ill, and an infection took her on February 8, 2015. She was the ultimate party girl, and led a vibrant and cultured life, so I still struggle to believe she's really gone from the world. Since her departure, I have deeply grieved my mother's loss. My experiences from 14 years ago, however, somewhat tempered me. I expected and recognized the intense fatigue and weariness that I still feel, and the unexpected crying jags don't frighten me. I knew going into this journey of grief, that any feelings were acceptable and normal, and so manifested a comparatively gentle grief experience. I chalk some of this mildness up to my choices: I haven't fought it, nor have I apologized or become upset with myself for it. When I need to be alone and do nothing, I do that. The one thing that's been quite comforting has been to watch classic movies and television shows, like my mom and I used to do.

The collective experience of mourning can deepen the impact of a loss. While I negotiated life without my mother, I watched my own daughter bitterly lament the loss of her grandmother. Additionally, I watched my mom's grandchildren, great grandsons, and my sister, endure the agony of her sudden exit. Watching the world continue to pitch forward, even though it was missing a key person in our lives, which included watching my esteemed and beloved stepfather remarry, magnified the pain of her absence.

Additionally, on the subject of grief-by-proxy, far too many of my friends have lost their children during these 14 years. Bearing witness and providing what little support I could while my friends have had to navigate the experience that is burying their own children, has been grueling. As a mother myself, I cannot imagine this particular kind of unfathomable, excruciating grief. My empathy and love for my bereaved friends has ensured that I don't come away from these losses completely unscathed, nor would I want it to.

Grief is a tender thread which has woven itself into the rich tapestry of my daily life and tethers me to those I have so treasured and lost.

"How lucky I am to have something that makes saying good-bye so hard."
A.A. Milne

Dedication

Firstly, I dedicate this book to Katherine and Chad, who were both old enough to understand, and strong enough to endure an absent mother. You were respectful in your expressions of anger at my absence, and empathetic in your responses. You've walked through your own grief, and you amaze me. I love you and treasure you both in my heart.

To John, my dear friend. You dropped everything when I called you, rescued me in my crisis by dealing with a client then came to comfort me. You didn't say a word; you just held me while I sobbed. I got tears, snot, and mascara all over your t-shirt, which was never the same. You didn't mind, and you didn't rush me or tell me how to feel. The world needs more people like you.

To Stephanie, the epitome of all that is good and proper. You always know exactly what to say and do. You were my daily lifeline, *patiently* reassuring me that I was not losing my mind, that I wouldn't be depressed for the rest of my life, and you reminded me often that something good could rise of all my pain. You were right.

To Wendy, You walked your own lonely path of anguish a few years before I did, when you lost your mother. I admire you so much. You read, search, and look for meaning in everything, no matter how difficult. Your ability to articulate and even joke about dark realities and to offer practical suggestions was invaluable to me. You just get me, and I know that is no easy feat.

Printed in the United States
By Bookmasters